Table Of Contents

Chapter 1: Introduction to Amazon Publishing

Understanding Amazon Publishing

Amazon Publishing has emerged as a game-changer in the world of self-publishing, providing a platform for authors to reach a global audience and gain recognition for their work. In this subchapter, we will delve into the intricacies of Amazon Publishing and how it can benefit online entrepreneurs and Kindle Direct Publishing (KDP) authors.

Amazon Publishing is a division of Amazon that allows authors to self-publish their books in both print and digital formats. It offers various publishing options, such as Kindle Direct Publishing (KDP), Amazon Publishing's imprints, and Amazon Publishing's partner programs. Understanding these options is crucial for entrepreneurs looking to establish a successful publishing career.

For online entrepreneurs, Amazon Publishing offers a unique opportunity to monetize their expertise by publishing books in their niche. By sharing their knowledge and experiences through a book, entrepreneurs can establish themselves as thought leaders and attract a wider audience. Additionally, Amazon Publishing provides robust marketing tools and resources to promote and sell their books to millions of potential readers.

Kindle Direct Publishing (KDP), the self-publishing platform by Amazon, allows authors to publish eBooks and paperbacks on the Kindle Store. It offers a simple and user-friendly interface, enabling authors to control every aspect of their book's publication process, from formatting to cover design. KDP authors can earn up to 70% royalties on eBook sales and expand their reach globally with Amazon's extensive distribution network.

Authors aspiring to gain more exposure and recognition can also explore Amazon Publishing's imprints. These imprints are specialized publishing houses under the Amazon umbrella that focus on specific genres or audiences. Getting published under an Amazon imprint can provide authors with additional marketing support, increased visibility, and a higher chance of landing traditional publishing deals.

Furthermore, Amazon Publishing's partner programs, such as Kindle Scout and Kindle Vella, offer authors alternative avenues to publish their work. Kindle Scout is a reader-powered publishing platform where readers nominate and vote for their favorite unpublished books, giving authors a chance to secure a publishing contract. Kindle Vella is a serialized storytelling platform that allows authors to publish stories in episodes, attracting readers who prefer bite-sized content.

In conclusion, understanding Amazon Publishing is crucial for online entrepreneurs and KDP authors looking to establish their presence in the publishing industry. By leveraging the various publishing options, entrepreneurs can monetize their expertise and gain recognition, while authors can reach a global audience and potentially secure traditional publishing deals. With Amazon's vast resources and marketing tools, the possibilities for success in Amazon Publishing are endless.

Benefits of Amazon Publishing for Entrepreneurs

In today's digital age, Amazon has become the go-to platform for entrepreneurs looking to publish and distribute their own books. With its vast reach and user-friendly publishing tools, Amazon Publishing offers a wide range of benefits for online entrepreneurs and Kindle Direct Publishing (KDP) authors. In this subchapter, we will explore some of the key advantages that Amazon Publishing provides for entrepreneurs.

1. Global Distribution: One of the most significant benefits of Amazon Publishing is its global reach. With millions of customers across the globe, Amazon allows entrepreneurs to tap into a vast international market. Through its various publishing options, including Kindle eBooks and print-on-demand services, entrepreneurs can expand their business beyond borders and connect with readers from all corners of the world.

2. Easy Publishing Process: Amazon Publishing provides entrepreneurs with a straightforward and user-friendly publishing process. Whether you are a first-time author or an experienced entrepreneur, Amazon's tools and resources make it easy to format and publish your book. The Kindle Direct Publishing platform allows you to upload your manuscript, design your cover, and set your own pricing in just a few simple steps.

3. Higher Royalties: Unlike traditional publishing models, Amazon Publishing offers higher royalty rates for authors. With the ability to earn up to 70% royalty on eBook sales and competitive rates for print-on-demand books, entrepreneurs can generate a more substantial income from their published works. This increased earning potential provides a lucrative avenue for entrepreneurs to monetize their knowledge and expertise.

4. Author Control: Amazon Publishing empowers entrepreneurs by giving them full control over their publishing journey. Authors can choose their own publishing timeline, make changes to their books whenever they want, and retain ownership of their intellectual property. This level of control allows entrepreneurs to adapt and respond to market demands quickly, ensuring their books remain relevant and profitable.

5. Enhanced Discoverability: With Amazon's powerful search algorithms and marketing tools, entrepreneurs can significantly improve their book's discoverability. By optimizing keywords, utilizing Amazon's advertising options, and leveraging the platform's promotional features, entrepreneurs can increase their book's visibility and attract a larger audience. This increased exposure can lead to higher sales and greater recognition for entrepreneurs in their respective niches.

In conclusion, Amazon Publishing offers a host of advantages for online entrepreneurs and Kindle Direct Publishing (KDP) authors. From global distribution and easy publishing processes to higher royalties and author control, Amazon provides entrepreneurs with the tools and platform they need to succeed in the publishing industry. By leveraging these benefits, entrepreneurs can reach a wider audience, monetize their knowledge, and establish themselves as industry experts. Whether you are a seasoned entrepreneur or just starting your journey, Amazon Publishing is a must-have resource for anyone looking to thrive in the digital publishing world.

Chapter 2: Getting Started with Kindle Direct Publishing (KDP)

What is Kindle Direct Publishing (KDP)?

In today's digital age, self-publishing has become a game-changer for aspiring authors and online entrepreneurs. Kindle Direct Publishing (KDP) is a platform offered by Amazon that allows authors to publish and distribute their books directly to millions of Kindle users worldwide.

KDP provides a unique opportunity for online entrepreneurs and authors in the Amazon Publishing niche to unleash their creativity, reach a global audience, and potentially generate substantial revenue. With KDP, authors have complete control over their work, from the content to the pricing and distribution strategy.

One of the key benefits of KDP is its simplicity. The platform provides an intuitive interface that makes it easy to upload and format your manuscript, design your book cover, and set the pricing. Whether you're a seasoned author or just starting your writing journey, KDP offers a user-friendly experience.

Once your book is published on KDP, it becomes available for purchase on the Kindle store, which is accessible to millions of readers worldwide. This means that your book has the potential to reach a vast audience, significantly expanding your readership and potential sales.

In addition to the global reach, KDP offers various promotional tools to help authors boost their book's visibility. These tools include Kindle Countdown Deals, Kindle Unlimited, and Kindle Free Book Promotions. Leveraging these features can drive more downloads, reviews, and ultimately increase your book's ranking on the Kindle store.

Another advantage of KDP is its flexible royalty structure. Authors can choose between two royalty options: the 35% royalty rate or the 70% royalty rate. The latter is available for books priced between $2.99 and $9.99, and it provides authors with a higher profit margin.

To maximize your success on KDP, it's crucial to have a well-defined marketing strategy. This involves optimizing your book description, utilizing keywords, engaging with readers through social media, and seeking reviews from reputable sources. The Ultimate Guide to Amazon Publishing: A Must-Have for Entrepreneurs provides valuable insights and strategies to help you navigate the world of KDP effectively.

In conclusion, Kindle Direct Publishing (KDP) is a powerful platform that empowers online entrepreneurs and authors in the Amazon Publishing niche to bring their books to life and reach a global audience. By leveraging the tools and resources provided by KDP, authors can turn their passion for writing into a profitable venture.

Creating a KDP Account

For any aspiring author or entrepreneur looking to publish their work on Amazon, creating a Kindle Direct Publishing (KDP) account is an essential first step. KDP provides a platform for authors to self-publish their books and reach a wide audience of readers worldwide. In this subchapter, we will guide you through the process of setting up your KDP account, ensuring that you have everything you need to start your publishing journey on Amazon.

To begin, visit the KDP website and click on the "Sign up" button. You will be prompted to enter your Amazon account credentials or create a new account if you don't already have one. Once you've logged in, you will be taken to the KDP dashboard, where you can manage all aspects of your publishing journey.

Next, it's time to set up your author profile. This is an important step as it helps readers connect with you and learn more about your work. Fill in your author name, biography, and add a high-quality author photo that represents your brand. Make sure to provide accurate and engaging information to entice readers to explore your books further.

After setting up your author profile, it's time to add your book. Click on "Create a new Kindle eBook" and follow the step-by-step instructions to input your book's title, subtitle, and description. You will also need to upload your book cover and manuscript files in the appropriate formats. KDP provides helpful guidelines to ensure your files meet their formatting requirements.

Once your book details are entered, you can set your pricing, choose whether to enroll your book in Kindle Unlimited or Kindle Select programs, and select the territories where you want your book to be available. Take your time to consider these options carefully, as they can impact your book's visibility and potential earnings.

Finally, it's time to hit the publish button. Congratulations! Your book will now go through a review process by the KDP team to ensure it meets their content guidelines. This usually takes around 24-48 hours. Once approved, your book will be available for purchase on Amazon's Kindle store, and you can start promoting and marketing your work to reach your target audience.

Creating a KDP account is the first step towards becoming a successful Amazon author. Take the time to set up your profile, add your book, and make informed decisions about pricing and enrollment. With the right strategy and dedication, KDP can be a powerful platform to reach a wide range of readers and grow your author brand. Good luck on your publishing journey!

Setting Up Your Author Profile

Your author profile is an essential tool for success in the world of Amazon publishing. It serves as your online identity and helps readers connect with you and your work. In this subchapter, we will guide you through the process of setting up a compelling author profile that will attract readers and boost your credibility as an author.

Firstly, it is crucial to understand the significance of a well-crafted author bio. This is your opportunity to showcase your expertise and build trust with your audience. Think of it as your elevator pitch – a concise and engaging summary of who you are as an author. Highlight your accomplishments, interests, and any relevant credentials that establish your authority in your niche. Remember to keep it concise, around 200-300 words, and write in a friendly, approachable tone.

Next, let's discuss the importance of a professional author photo. Readers are more likely to connect with a face rather than an anonymous name. Invest in a high-quality headshot that reflects your personality and aligns with your brand. Dress appropriately, smile, and maintain good eye contact. A captivating author photo can make a lasting impression and help readers relate to you on a personal level.

Additionally, take advantage of the Amazon Author Central platform. This powerful tool allows you to manage your author profile across all Amazon marketplaces. It offers features like updating your bio, adding photos, and even integrating your blog posts. Regularly update your author profile to keep it fresh and engaging. Be sure to link your social media accounts and website to further connect with your audience.

Lastly, leverage customer reviews to enhance your author profile. Positive reviews build credibility and attract potential readers. Encourage readers to leave reviews by including a call-to-action at the end of your books. Engage with your readers by responding to their reviews and addressing any concerns they may have. This interaction shows that you value their feedback and are invested in creating a positive reading experience.

In conclusion, setting up your author profile is a vital step in building a successful Amazon publishing career. Craft a compelling author bio, choose a professional author photo, utilize the Amazon Author Central platform, and engage with your readers through customer reviews. By following these guidelines, you will establish a strong online presence, connect with your target audience, and ultimately increase your chances of success as an author in the competitive world of Amazon publishing.

Chapter 3: Writing and Formatting Your Book

Choosing the Right Topic for Your Book

When it comes to publishing a book on Amazon, choosing the right topic is crucial for success. As an online entrepreneur or entrepreneur in the niche of Amazon Publishing or Kindle Direct Publishing (KDP) authors, you understand the importance of selecting a topic that resonates with your target audience and stands out in a crowded marketplace. This subchapter will guide you through the process of finding the perfect topic for your book, ensuring it appeals to readers and maximizes your chances of success.

First and foremost, consider your passion and expertise. Writing about a topic you are genuinely interested in and knowledgeable about will not only make the writing process enjoyable but also help you connect with your readers on a deeper level. Your enthusiasm will shine through your words, making your book more engaging and valuable to your audience.

Next, conduct thorough market research. Look for popular and trending topics that align with your passions and expertise. Explore bestseller lists, search keywords on Amazon, and read customer reviews to gain insights into what readers are currently looking for and what gaps exist in the market. By identifying these gaps, you can position yourself as an authority and fill the demand with your unique perspective.

Additionally, consider the profitability of your chosen topic. While passion is essential, it is equally important to ensure your book has the potential to generate sales. Analyze the competition and assess the market demand for your topic. Are there other books already covering the subject? If so, what can you offer that is different or better? Finding a balance between your passion and market demand will increase your chances of success.

Moreover, consider your target audience. Who are they, and what are their interests and needs? Understanding your ideal reader will guide you in selecting a topic that appeals to them and provides value. Consider conducting surveys or engaging with your audience on social media platforms to gather insights and better understand their preferences.

Finally, be flexible and open to feedback. As an author, you should be willing to adapt and evolve. Pay attention to reader feedback, reviews, and market trends. Use this information to refine your topic or explore new directions for future books. Adaptability is key to staying relevant and successful in the ever-changing world of Amazon Publishing.

By carefully selecting the right topic for your book, you set yourself up for success in the competitive world of Amazon Publishing. Remember to consider your passion, market demand, profitability, and target audience while remaining open to feedback and adaptation. With these strategies, you can create a book that resonates with readers and maximizes your entrepreneurial potential.

Writing Compelling Content

In the ever-expanding world of online entrepreneurship, creating compelling content is a skill that can set you apart from the competition. In this subchapter, we will delve into the art of crafting captivating content for Amazon Publishing and Kindle Direct Publishing (KDP) authors. Whether you are a seasoned writer or just starting out, mastering this vital skill will be essential for your success.

The key to writing compelling content lies in understanding your target audience. As an online entrepreneur, you must have a deep understanding of who you are writing for. Conduct thorough market research to identify the needs, desires, and pain points of your specific niche within Amazon Publishing and KDP authors. This will enable you to create content that resonates with your audience and keeps them engaged.

Once you have a clear understanding of your target audience, it's time to focus on your writing style. Compelling content is not just about conveying information; it's about creating an emotional connection with your readers. Use storytelling techniques to captivate your audience and make your content relatable. Incorporate personal experiences, anecdotes, and examples that your readers can connect with on an emotional level.

Another crucial aspect of writing compelling content is providing value to your readers. Your content should offer practical tips, insights, or solutions to their problems. Demonstrate your expertise in the field of Amazon Publishing or KDP authorship by providing actionable advice that your audience can implement immediately. This will establish you as a trusted authority and keep readers coming back for more.

In addition to providing value, it's essential to make your content visually appealing. Use bullet points, subheadings, and concise paragraphs to break up your content and make it easier to read. Incorporate relevant images, infographics, or videos to enhance the overall presentation and engage your audience visually.

Lastly, don't forget to optimize your content for search engines. Conduct keyword research to identify popular search terms within your niche and incorporate them naturally throughout your content. This will increase your visibility on platforms like Amazon and help you attract a wider audience.

In conclusion, writing compelling content is a crucial skill for online entrepreneurs in the Amazon Publishing and KDP authorship niches. By understanding your target audience, creating an emotional connection, providing value, and optimizing for search engines, you can create content that captivates readers and drives success. Mastering this skill will not only enhance your online presence but also establish you as a trusted authority within your niche.

Editing and Proofreading Your Book

As an online entrepreneur and author in the realm of Amazon publishing and Kindle Direct Publishing (KDP), it is crucial to recognize the significance of editing and proofreading your book. These essential steps ensure that your work is polished, error-free, and ready to captivate readers. In this subchapter, we will delve into the art of editing and proofreading, equipping you with the knowledge and tools you need to elevate the quality of your book.

Editing is the process of refining your manuscript, addressing structural issues, improving clarity, and enhancing the overall readability of your work. It involves reviewing your book from a macro perspective, focusing on plot development, character arcs, pacing, and consistency. As an online entrepreneur, it is imperative to comprehend the impact of a well-edited book on your readership and sales potential. Engaging the services of a professional editor or leveraging editing software can significantly improve the quality of your book.

Proofreading, on the other hand, is the final step before publication, focusing on grammar, spelling, punctuation, and formatting errors. It is the meticulous examination of your book at a micro level, ensuring that every sentence is flawless and error-free. While proofreading can be done by yourself, it is advisable to engage a fresh set of eyes, as they can spot mistakes that you might have overlooked.

To effectively edit and proofread your book, here are some essential tips to follow:

1. Take a break: After completing the initial draft, step away from your book for a few days or weeks. This break will help you approach the editing process with a fresh perspective.

2. Create a checklist: Develop a comprehensive checklist of items to review during the editing and proofreading process. This will help you stay organized and ensure that no aspect is overlooked.

3. Seek professional help: Consider hiring a professional editor who specializes in your genre or utilizing editing software to enhance the quality of your book. Their expertise will undoubtedly elevate your work to a new level.

4. Engage beta readers: Enlist the help of beta readers who can provide valuable feedback on your book's content, structure, and overall appeal. Their insights can be invaluable in improving your manuscript.

5. Proofread meticulously: Pay attention to every detail, from grammar and punctuation to formatting and consistency. Use online tools and resources to aid in this process and consider working with a professional proofreader for a final review.

By investing time and effort into editing and proofreading your book, you demonstrate your commitment to delivering a top-notch reading experience to your audience. This attention to detail will undoubtedly set you apart as an online entrepreneur in the competitive world of Amazon publishing and Kindle Direct Publishing (KDP).

Formatting Your Book for Kindle

When it comes to publishing your book on Amazon, one crucial step is formatting it for Kindle. Kindle Direct Publishing (KDP) is an excellent platform for self-publishing authors, and understanding how to properly format your book for Kindle can significantly impact its success. In this subchapter, we will guide you through the essential steps and best practices for formatting your book for Kindle.

First and foremost, it is crucial to ensure your book's content is properly organized. Start by creating a table of contents that includes links to each chapter or section of your book. This allows readers to navigate easily through your book and enhances their reading experience. Additionally, consider breaking down your book into smaller sections or chapters to improve readability on Kindle devices.

Next, pay close attention to the formatting of your text. Keep in mind that Kindle devices have different screen sizes, so it is important to choose a font and font size that is easily readable on all devices. Avoid using elaborate fonts or font sizes that are too small, as this can strain the reader's eyes. Stick to a clean, simple font that is legible across various Kindle devices.

Another crucial aspect of formatting your book for Kindle is ensuring proper spacing. Kindle readers prefer a comfortable reading experience, and excessive spacing or cramped text can be off-putting. Use consistent paragraph spacing and avoid using multiple spaces between paragraphs. Additionally, ensure that your text is aligned properly, with consistent margins throughout the book.

Graphics and images can add visual appeal to your book, but it is essential to optimize them for Kindle devices. Ensure that images are high-quality and properly sized for Kindle screens. Compress the images to reduce file size and choose the appropriate file format, such as JPEG or PNG, for optimal display on Kindle devices.

Lastly, before publishing your book, thoroughly test it on various Kindle devices and apps. This step allows you to identify any formatting inconsistencies or errors that may impact the reading experience. Take the time to fix any issues and make necessary adjustments to ensure your book looks professional and well-formatted across all Kindle platforms.

By following these formatting guidelines, you can enhance the readability and overall presentation of your book on Kindle. A well-formatted book not only provides a positive reading experience but also increases the likelihood of positive reviews and recommendations. Take the time to properly format your book for Kindle, and you will be one step closer to success as an Amazon Publishing author.

Chapter 4: Designing an Eye-Catching Book Cover

Importance of a Professional Book Cover

In the competitive world of online publishing, first impressions are everything. As an online entrepreneur or author on Amazon Publishing or Kindle Direct Publishing (KDP), the importance of a professional book cover cannot be overstated. It is the face of your book, the first thing potential readers see, and ultimately, the key to gaining attention, attracting readers, and increasing sales.

One of the main reasons why a professional book cover is crucial is because it captures the essence of your book and communicates it to the audience effectively. A well-designed cover has the ability to convey the genre, tone, and overall mood of your book at a glance. Whether it's a romance novel, a self-help guide, or a thrilling mystery, a professional cover tells potential readers what to expect and entices them to explore further.

Furthermore, a professional book cover helps your book stand out in a sea of other titles. On platforms like Amazon, where thousands of books are published every day, it's essential to have a cover that catches the eye amidst the competition. A visually appealing and professionally designed cover sets your book apart, making it more likely to be noticed, clicked on, and ultimately purchased.

Additionally, a professional book cover conveys a sense of credibility and professionalism. Just like a shoddy storefront can deter customers from entering a physical store, a poorly designed cover can make potential readers question the quality of the content inside. On the other hand, a professionally crafted cover signals that the author has invested time and effort into their work, suggesting a well-written and polished book.

Moreover, a professional book cover enhances discoverability. When readers are browsing through online platforms, they often rely on visual cues to guide their choices. A captivating cover can attract readers who might not have been actively searching for a book in your genre, expanding your potential audience and increasing the chances of your book being discovered by new readers.

In conclusion, for online entrepreneurs and authors in the world of Amazon Publishing or Kindle Direct Publishing (KDP), a professional book cover is an indispensable element of success. It not only captures the essence of your book but also helps it stand out, conveys credibility, and enhances discoverability. Putting in the effort to create or hire a professional designer for your book cover is a small investment that can yield enormous returns in terms of attracting readers, increasing sales, and establishing your reputation as a serious author.

Hiring a Graphic Designer

In today's digital age, visual appeal plays a crucial role in attracting and engaging readers. Whether you are an online entrepreneur or a Kindle Direct Publishing (KDP) author, having a professional-looking book cover, website design, or promotional materials can make a world of difference in capturing your target audience's attention. This is where hiring a skilled graphic designer becomes essential.

A graphic designer is a creative professional specializing in visual communication. They possess the expertise to transform your ideas into visually stunning designs that enhance your brand and effectively convey your message. Here are a few reasons why hiring a graphic designer can be a game-changer for your Amazon publishing journey.

Firstly, a graphic designer brings a fresh perspective to your project. They have an eye for aesthetics and can provide innovative ideas that you may not have considered. By collaborating with a designer, you can tap into their creative expertise and ensure that your book cover or promotional materials stand out from the competition.

Secondly, a graphic designer possesses technical skills and knowledge of design principles that can take your visuals to the next level. They are proficient in using industry-standard software and tools to create high-quality designs that are visually appealing and optimized for various platforms. Whether it's creating an eye-catching book cover or designing a user-friendly website, a graphic designer knows how to strike the right balance between functionality and aesthetics.

Moreover, hiring a graphic designer saves you valuable time and effort. As an entrepreneur, your focus should be on creating content, marketing strategies, and growing your business. By delegating the design tasks to a professional, you can free up your time to concentrate on what you do best while ensuring that your visual assets are handled by an expert.

When hiring a graphic designer, it's essential to consider their portfolio, experience, and expertise in your niche. Look for designers who have worked with Amazon publishing or KDP authors before, as they will have a better understanding of the specific requirements and trends in the industry.

In conclusion, hiring a graphic designer is a worthwhile investment for online entrepreneurs and Amazon publishing authors. Their creative vision, technical skills, and efficiency can elevate your visuals and enhance your brand's overall appeal. By collaborating with a graphic designer, you can create visually stunning designs that captivate your target audience and give your Amazon publishing journey a competitive edge.

Designing Your Book Cover on Your Own

When it comes to self-publishing your book on Amazon, one of the most critical aspects that can make or break its success is the book cover design. A well-designed book cover not only grabs attention but also conveys the essence of your book, enticing potential readers to click and explore further. While hiring a professional designer is always an option, designing your book cover on your own can be a cost-effective and rewarding experience, especially for online entrepreneurs and Kindle Direct Publishing (KDP) authors.

Before diving into the design process, it's essential to understand the key elements that make a book cover visually appealing and effective. The cover should reflect the genre and tone of your book, using appropriate typography, color schemes, imagery, and layout. Researching successful book covers in your niche can provide inspiration and help you understand the elements that resonate with your target audience.

The first step in designing your book cover is choosing the right software. There are various graphic design tools available, both free and paid, that can help you bring your creative vision to life. Popular options include Canva, Adobe Photoshop, and GIMP. These tools offer user-friendly interfaces, pre-designed templates, and extensive libraries of fonts and images.

Once you have selected your software, start by brainstorming ideas and sketches for your book cover. Consider the themes, motifs, and symbols that represent your book's content. Experiment with different layouts, fonts, and color combinations to find the perfect balance that captures the essence of your story.

Next, focus on typography. Choose fonts that are legible, visually appealing, and align with your book's genre. Play with font styles, sizes, and placements to create a captivating title and author name. Remember, simplicity is key; an overcrowded cover can be overwhelming and unattractive.

When it comes to imagery, high-quality visuals are essential. If you're adept at graphic design, you can create your own custom illustrations or photography. However, for those without design skills, stock image websites like Shutterstock and Unsplash offer a vast selection of affordable and royalty-free images.

After finalizing your design, gather feedback from trusted individuals, such as fellow authors or potential readers. Their insights can help you fine-tune any aspects of your book cover that may need improvement.

In conclusion, designing your book cover on your own can be a rewarding and cost-effective way for online entrepreneurs and KDP authors to create visually appealing covers that resonate with their target audience. By understanding the key design elements, utilizing appropriate software, and experimenting with typography and imagery, you can craft a book cover that entices readers and enhances the overall success of your book on Amazon. So, roll up your sleeves and let your creativity flow – the perfect book cover awaits!

Chapter 5: Publishing Your Book on Amazon

Uploading Your Book to KDP

Once you have finished writing and editing your book, it's time to take the next crucial step: uploading it to Kindle Direct Publishing (KDP) on Amazon. In this subchapter, we will guide you through the process of uploading your book to KDP, ensuring that it is ready for publication and available to millions of readers worldwide.

First, it is essential to create an account on KDP if you haven't already. KDP is Amazon's self-publishing platform, and it offers a seamless and user-friendly experience for authors. Once you have signed up, you'll be directed to your KDP dashboard, where you can manage all aspects of your book's publication.

Before uploading your book, make sure you have prepared the necessary files. KDP accepts manuscripts in several formats, including Word documents, ePub, and PDF. Ensure that your manuscript is properly formatted, with consistent headers, footers, and chapter breaks. Pay attention to the font, spacing, and margins to ensure a professional-looking final product.

Next, you'll need to create a new title on KDP. Provide all the relevant details, such as the book's title, author name, and book description. Add keywords and categories that accurately represent your book's genre and content, as this will help readers find your book in relevant searches.

Now it's time to upload your book file. Follow KDP's step-by-step instructions to select the appropriate file format and upload your manuscript. KDP will automatically convert your file into a Kindle-compatible format, but it's still crucial to preview the converted version to ensure it looks as intended. You can also enable the "Look Inside" feature, allowing potential readers to preview a portion of your book before making a purchase.

After uploading your manuscript, you'll need to create a cover for your book. KDP provides a cover creator tool that allows you to design a professional-looking cover using their templates. Alternatively, you can hire a professional book cover designer to create a unique and eye-catching cover that attracts readers.

Once your manuscript and cover are uploaded, you can set the pricing and distribution options for your book. Decide whether you want to enroll your book in KDP Select, a program that offers exclusive promotional opportunities and higher royalties. You can also choose the territories where you want your book to be available and set the royalty rates for each.

Finally, review all the information you have provided and click on the "Publish" button. Congratulations! Your book is now live on Amazon, and readers can start discovering and purchasing it.

Remember, successfully uploading your book to KDP is just the beginning of your self-publishing journey. Promote your book through various marketing strategies, engage with your readers, and continuously improve your writing skills to ensure long-term success as an Amazon publishing author.

Setting the Right Price for Your Book

As an online entrepreneur and a Kindle Direct Publishing (KDP) author, one of the most critical decisions you will make is setting the right price for your book. Pricing plays a crucial role in the success of your book, as it directly impacts your sales, revenue, and overall profitability. In this subchapter, we will explore the factors you need to consider when determining the optimal price for your book on Amazon Publishing.

First and foremost, it's essential to research the market and understand the pricing trends in your niche. Analyze the prices of similar books, both traditionally published and self-published, to get a sense of the average price range. This will help you position your book competitively while taking into account its unique value proposition.

Consider the length, genre, and target audience of your book. Longer books or those in specialized niches might command higher prices, while shorter books or those aimed at a broader audience may benefit from a lower price point. Understanding your readers' preferences and their willingness to pay for your content will assist you in making an informed decision.

Another crucial factor to consider is your goals for publishing your book. Are you primarily looking to make a profit, build your author brand, or establish yourself as an expert in your field? Each of these objectives may require a different pricing strategy. For example, if your goal is to gain visibility and attract a large readership, setting a lower price or even offering your book for free temporarily can help generate buzz and attract potential readers.

Furthermore, take into account the pricing options available on Amazon Publishing. With KDP Select, you have the option to enroll your book in Kindle Unlimited (KU) and Kindle Owners' Lending Library (KOLL), where readers can borrow your book for free. This can be a valuable strategy to increase your book's visibility and reach a wider audience. However, it also affects your royalties, so carefully weigh the pros and cons before deciding.

Lastly, don't forget to periodically review and adjust your pricing strategy. The market is dynamic, and reader preferences change over time. Monitoring your book's sales, reviews, and rankings will provide valuable insights into whether your current pricing strategy is effective or if adjustments are needed.

Setting the right price for your book on Amazon Publishing is a delicate balancing act. By considering market trends, your book's characteristics, your goals, and the available pricing options, you can make an informed decision that maximizes your book's potential for success. Remember, pricing is not set in stone, and regularly evaluating and adapting your strategy will help you stay ahead in the competitive world of Amazon Publishing.

Choosing Kindle Select or Going Wide

For online entrepreneurs and Kindle Direct Publishing (KDP) authors, one of the most crucial decisions to make is whether to enroll their eBooks in Kindle Select or go wide. Kindle Select is an exclusive program offered by Amazon that requires authors to make their eBooks available exclusively on the Kindle platform for a period of 90 days, while going wide means distributing eBooks across multiple platforms, such as Barnes & Noble, Kobo, and Apple Books.

The decision between Kindle Select and going wide depends on various factors that authors must carefully consider. Let's explore the benefits and drawbacks of each option to help entrepreneurs make an informed choice.

Kindle Select offers several advantages. Firstly, it allows authors to take advantage of Kindle Unlimited (KU) and the Kindle Owners' Lending Library (KOLL). These programs enable readers to borrow and read eBooks for free, providing authors with additional income through the Kindle Unlimited Global Fund. Moreover, authors enrolled in Kindle Select can promote their eBooks using Kindle Countdown Deals and Free Book Promotions, which can significantly boost visibility and sales.

However, choosing Kindle Select also means giving up the opportunity to distribute eBooks on other platforms. Going wide allows authors to reach a broader audience, tapping into different eBook markets and potentially increasing sales. Additionally, by diversifying distribution, authors reduce their dependence on a single platform and mitigate the risk of losing all their income if they encounter issues with Amazon.

To make an informed decision, entrepreneurs need to consider their goals and priorities. If maximizing income through Kindle Unlimited reads and utilizing Amazon's promotional tools is a primary focus, Kindle Select may be the right choice. Conversely, if authors prioritize reaching a wider audience and diversifying their income streams, going wide is a better option.

It is worth noting that authors can experiment with both approaches. By initially enrolling in Kindle Select for the first 90 days, authors can assess the benefits of the program. If the results are promising, they can continue with Kindle Select; otherwise, they can choose to go wide afterward.

Ultimately, the decision between Kindle Select and going wide is a strategic one that should align with an author's specific goals and circumstances. By carefully weighing the advantages and disadvantages of each approach, online entrepreneurs and KDP authors can optimize their eBook publishing journey and maximize their potential for success.

Publishing Your Book in Paperback

For online entrepreneurs and authors in the Amazon Publishing and Kindle Direct Publishing (KDP) niches, venturing into the world of paperback publishing can be a lucrative opportunity. While e-books dominate the digital market, there is still a significant demand for physical copies of books. In this subchapter, we will explore the process of publishing your book in paperback, providing you with valuable insights and practical tips to make your journey a success.

The first step in publishing your book in paperback is formatting. Unlike e-books, the layout and design of a paperback require careful attention to detail. Ensure that your manuscript is properly formatted with appropriate fonts, margins, and line spacing. Consider hiring a professional formatter or utilizing software tools specifically designed for paperback formatting.

Next, you will need to create a captivating book cover. A visually appealing cover is crucial for attracting potential readers. Remember, people do judge books by their covers. Invest in a professional graphic designer who can create a visually stunning and marketable book cover that accurately represents your book's content and genre.

Once your manuscript is formatted and your cover is ready, it's time to choose a printing and distribution solution. Amazon's KDP platform offers a Print-on-Demand (POD) service, allowing you to print and distribute your paperback books without upfront costs or inventory. Take advantage of this service to reach a global audience and maximize your sales potential.

Before officially publishing your book, proofread and edit it thoroughly. Typos and grammatical errors can negatively affect your book's credibility and professionalism. Consider hiring a professional editor or utilizing professional editing software to ensure your book is error-free and ready for publication.

Once your paperback is published, focus on marketing and promotion. Leverage your existing online presence and social media platforms to create buzz around your book. Engage with potential readers, offer discounts or giveaways, and seek out opportunities for book reviews and author interviews. Utilize Amazon's marketing tools, such as Kindle Countdown Deals and Kindle Unlimited, to reach a wider audience and boost your sales.

Lastly, continuously monitor and analyze your book's performance. Pay attention to customer reviews and feedback, adjusting your marketing strategies accordingly. Experiment with different pricing options, book descriptions, and keywords to optimize your book's visibility and generate more sales.

Publishing your book in paperback can be a highly rewarding endeavor for online entrepreneurs and authors in the Amazon Publishing and KDP niches. By following the steps outlined in this subchapter and consistently refining your strategies, you can effectively tap into the demand for physical books and achieve success in the ever-evolving publishing industry.

Chapter 6: Marketing and Promoting Your Book

Building a Strong Author Platform

In the ever-evolving landscape of the publishing industry, having a strong author platform is essential for success. As an online entrepreneur or an entrepreneur in the Amazon Publishing and Kindle Direct Publishing (KDP) niche, understanding how to build and leverage your author platform is crucial for reaching a wider audience and maximizing your book's potential.

An author platform is the sum total of your online presence, which includes your website, social media profiles, email list, and any other online channels that you utilize to connect with your readers. It is the foundation upon which you can build your brand, establish credibility, and cultivate a loyal following.

One of the first steps to building a strong author platform is creating a professional and engaging website. Your website should be visually appealing, easy to navigate, and contain essential information about you and your books. It should showcase your author bio, book summaries, reviews, and links to purchase your books. Additionally, consider starting a blog on your website where you can share valuable content related to your niche, engage with your readers, and demonstrate your expertise.

Social media platforms are powerful tools for authors to connect with their audience. Identify the platforms where your target readers spend their time and create engaging profiles. Regularly share updates about your books, behind-the-scenes insights, and interact with your followers. Building relationships with your readers through social media can help you gain valuable feedback, increase your book's visibility, and ultimately boost your sales.

Another crucial element of a strong author platform is building an email list. Offer incentives, such as exclusive content or freebies, to entice readers to subscribe to your list. By having direct access to your readers' inboxes, you can send personalized updates, book launch announcements, and promotions, fostering a deeper connection with your audience.

Collaborating with other authors and influencers in your niche can also help expand your author platform. Consider guest blogging on popular websites, participating in podcast interviews, or organizing joint promotions. By tapping into the existing audiences of others, you can gain exposure to new readers who share an interest in your genre or topic.

Finally, never underestimate the power of consistent and quality content. Whether it's through your blog, social media posts, or email newsletters, prioritize providing value to your audience. Share insights, tips, and behind-the-scenes stories that resonate with your readers and keep them engaged.

In conclusion, building a strong author platform is a vital step for online entrepreneurs and entrepreneurs in the Amazon Publishing and KDP niche. By creating an engaging website, leveraging social media, building an email list, collaborating with others, and consistently producing quality content, you can establish yourself as an authoritative and influential author, effectively reaching and connecting with your target audience.

Leveraging Social Media for Book Promotion

In today's digital age, social media has become an indispensable tool for promoting products, services, and even books. As an online entrepreneur or an author in the Amazon Publishing or Kindle Direct Publishing (KDP) niches, understanding how to effectively leverage social media for book promotion is crucial to your success.

Social media platforms offer a vast audience and a multitude of marketing opportunities. By utilizing these platforms strategically, you can connect with readers, build a loyal fan base, and drive sales for your books. Here are some key strategies to consider when leveraging social media for book promotion:

1. Choose the right platforms: Not all social media platforms are created equal, and each has its own unique user base and features. As an author, focus on platforms that cater to your target audience. For example, Facebook and Instagram are popular choices for engaging with readers, while LinkedIn may be more suitable for connecting with other authors or industry professionals.

2. Build an engaging online presence: Create an author page or profile that reflects your brand and showcases your books. Share compelling content, such as book excerpts, behind-the-scenes insights, and personal anecdotes. Engage with your audience by responding to comments and messages promptly, and foster a sense of community by encouraging discussions and feedback.

3. Utilize visual content: People are drawn to visually appealing content, so make use of eye-catching graphics, book covers, and promotional images. Share book trailers, author interviews, or live streams to generate buzz and capture the attention of potential readers. Platforms like Pinterest and YouTube can be particularly advantageous for showcasing visual content.

4. Collaborate with influencers and bloggers: Influencers and bloggers who have a substantial following in the book or publishing industry can help amplify your book's exposure. Partner with them to create sponsored posts, guest blog entries, or even host virtual book events together. Their endorsement can significantly increase your book's visibility and credibility.

5. Run targeted ads and promotions: Most social media platforms offer advertising features that allow you to target specific demographics and interests. Create compelling ad campaigns to reach your ideal readers. Additionally, consider running exclusive promotions or giveaways on social media to reward your followers and entice new readers to discover your books.

Remember to monitor your social media analytics regularly to assess the performance of your promotional efforts. Adjust your strategies accordingly and experiment with different approaches to find what resonates best with your audience.

By leveraging social media effectively, you can expand your reach, connect with readers, and drive book sales. Incorporate these strategies into your book promotion efforts, and watch as your online presence as an author flourishes.

Engaging with Readers and Building a Fanbase

In the world of Amazon Publishing and Kindle Direct Publishing (KDP), success goes beyond simply writing and publishing a book. To truly thrive as an author, it is essential to engage with readers and build a loyal fanbase. This subchapter aims to provide online entrepreneurs, particularly those in the Amazon Publishing and KDP niches, with valuable insights and strategies for connecting with readers and fostering a dedicated following.

One of the first steps to engage with readers is to establish a strong online presence. Utilize various social media platforms, such as Facebook, Instagram, and Twitter, to connect with potential readers and build relationships. Regularly post engaging content related to your book, share snippets, behind-the-scenes insights, and even personal anecdotes. Actively respond to comments and messages, showing genuine interest in your readers' opinions and feedback. By consistently engaging with your audience, you can create a sense of community and make readers feel valued.

Another effective way to connect with readers is through book signings, author events, and online book clubs. Organize events in local bookstores, libraries, or even virtual platforms, where you can interact directly with your audience. Encourage open discussions, answer questions, and provide a glimpse into your writing process. By meeting readers face-to-face, you can forge a personal connection that will resonate with them long after the event.

Building a fanbase also requires leveraging the power of email marketing. Develop a website or author page where readers can sign up for your newsletter. Offer exclusive content, such as bonus chapters, author interviews, or sneak peeks for upcoming projects, to entice readers to subscribe. Regularly send newsletters to your fanbase, keeping them updated about your work, upcoming events, and any exciting news related to your books. Cultivating a direct line of communication through email allows you to maintain a close relationship with your most dedicated readers.

Furthermore, consider collaborating with other authors or influencers in your niche. By guest blogging, participating in joint author interviews, or even co-writing books, you can tap into their existing fanbase and expand your own reach. Building connections with like-minded individuals can open doors to new opportunities and widen your readership.

In conclusion, engaging with readers and building a loyal fanbase is crucial for success in Amazon Publishing and KDP. By establishing an online presence, hosting events, utilizing email marketing, and collaborating with others, you can create a thriving community around your work. Remember, building a fanbase takes time and effort, but the rewards of having dedicated readers who eagerly await your next release are well worth it.

Utilizing Amazon Advertising and Promotions

When it comes to succeeding in the world of Amazon publishing, utilizing Amazon Advertising and Promotions is an essential tool in your arsenal. Whether you are an online entrepreneur or a Kindle Direct Publishing (KDP) author, understanding how to effectively leverage these platforms can significantly boost your sales and increase your visibility on Amazon.

Amazon Advertising is a powerful tool that allows you to reach a wider audience and promote your books to potential readers. With Amazon Advertising, you can create sponsored product ads, display ads, and even video ads to target specific keywords, genres, or customer interests. By strategically placing your ads, you can increase your book's visibility, drive more traffic to your product page, and ultimately boost your sales.

In addition to Amazon Advertising, Amazon Promotions offer a great way to generate buzz and attract new readers. With promotions such as Kindle Countdown Deals, Free Book Promotions, and Kindle Unlimited, you have the opportunity to reach a larger audience and entice them to try your book. These promotions not only help you increase your book's visibility but also allow you to gather valuable reviews and feedback, which can further enhance your credibility as an author.

To make the most of Amazon Advertising and Promotions, it is crucial to carefully plan your marketing strategy. Start by identifying your target audience and understanding their preferences and interests. Use this information to create compelling ad copy, eye-catching visuals, and enticing promotions that will resonate with your potential readers. Monitor your campaigns regularly and make necessary adjustments to optimize your results and maximize your return on investment.

Furthermore, don't forget to leverage the power of data and analytics provided by Amazon. Use these insights to track your ad performance, identify areas for improvement, and refine your marketing strategy. By constantly analyzing and adapting, you can stay ahead of your competition and continue to grow your author business on Amazon.

In conclusion, Amazon Advertising and Promotions are invaluable tools for online entrepreneurs and Kindle Direct Publishing authors. By intelligently utilizing these platforms, you can increase your book's visibility, attract more readers, and ultimately boost your sales. Stay proactive, continually refine your strategy, and watch your author business thrive in the world of Amazon publishing.

Chapter 7: Maximizing Sales and Reviews

Optimizing Your Book Description and Metadata

In the fast-paced world of online entrepreneurship, standing out from the crowd is crucial to success. For authors in the Amazon Publishing and Kindle Direct Publishing (KDP) niches, optimizing your book description and metadata can make all the difference in attracting potential readers and maximizing sales. In this subchapter, we will explore the essential strategies and techniques to optimize your book's description and metadata, ensuring it captures the attention of your target audience.

Your book description serves as your sales pitch, enticing readers to click the "Buy Now" button. It should be concise, compelling, and highlight the unique aspects of your book. Start with a powerful hook to grab attention and summarize your book's main theme or message. Use persuasive language and vivid descriptions to create an emotional connection with your readers. Remember, you have limited space, so make every word count.

Furthermore, don't forget to incorporate relevant keywords in your book description. Conduct thorough research to identify popular search terms related to your book's genre or topic. Including these keywords strategically can improve your book's visibility in Amazon's search results and attract more organic traffic.

Metadata, on the other hand, refers to the information you provide to categorize your book accurately. This includes selecting the most relevant categories and subcategories for your book, as well as choosing appropriate keywords. Take the time to analyze the categories that best align with your book's content and target audience. Selecting the right categories will ensure your book appears in relevant search results, increasing its discoverability.

When it comes to keywords, think like your audience. What words or phrases would they use to search for a book like yours? Aim for a mix of broader keywords and long-tail keywords specific to your book's niche. Tools like Amazon Keyword Research can help you discover popular keywords and phrases that resonate with your target audience.

Regularly monitoring and updating your book's metadata is crucial. Stay up-to-date with the latest trends, popular keywords, and changes in Amazon's algorithms. Consistently optimizing your metadata will boost your book's visibility, ultimately leading to increased sales and revenue.

In conclusion, optimizing your book description and metadata is an essential step in maximizing your book's potential as an Amazon Publishing or Kindle Direct Publishing author. By crafting a compelling book description, incorporating relevant keywords, and meticulously managing your metadata, you can significantly improve your book's discoverability and attract your target audience. Stay informed, experiment with different strategies, and continually refine your book's metadata to ensure your book stands out among the vast sea of online publications.

Generating Positive Reviews for Your Book

Subchapter: Generating Positive Reviews for Your Book

As an author, one of the most crucial aspects of promoting your book on Amazon is generating positive reviews. Positive reviews not only enhance your book's credibility but also act as a powerful marketing tool. In this subchapter, we will explore effective strategies for attracting and encouraging positive reviews for your book on Amazon.

1. Engage with Your Readers: Building a relationship with your readers is key to generating positive reviews. Engage with your audience through social media platforms, author websites, or email newsletters. By interacting with

your readers, you create a loyal fan base that is more likely to leave positive reviews.

2. Offer Advance Reader Copies (ARCs): Before your book's official release, provide free digital or physical copies to a select group of readers. These advance copies can be given to bloggers, influencers, or book clubs in exchange for honest reviews. Their feedback can help create buzz and increase anticipation for your book's launch.

3. Leverage Your Network: Reach out to friends, family, and colleagues who have read your book and ask them to leave an honest review on Amazon. Encourage them to be specific about what they enjoyed or found valuable in your writing. These initial reviews will establish credibility and encourage others to follow suit.

4. Utilize Author Central: Amazon's Author Central is a platform exclusively designed for authors. Take advantage of this tool by creating an engaging author bio, adding book trailers or relevant videos, and linking your blog or website. By showcasing your expertise and personality, you can attract more readers and, subsequently, more positive reviews.

5. Offer Incentives: Consider offering incentives to readers who leave reviews on Amazon. This could be in the form of exclusive bonus content, access to a private Facebook group, or entry into a giveaway. Incentives not only motivate readers to share their thoughts but also encourage them to recommend your book to others.

6. Encourage Book Clubs: Reach out to book clubs that align with your book's genre or topic and offer to participate in their discussions. Engaging with book clubs allows you to gain exposure among avid readers who are more likely to leave positive reviews. Additionally, their discussions can provide valuable insights for future book improvements.

Remember, while it's essential to generate positive reviews, it's equally important to respect Amazon's guidelines regarding review solicitation. Avoid incentivizing readers to leave positive reviews or engaging in fraudulent practices, as this can harm your reputation and potentially lead to penalties from Amazon.

By implementing these strategies and consistently delivering high-quality content, you can generate a strong base of positive reviews for your book on Amazon. Positive reviews not only boost sales but also establish you as a reputable author, ultimately leading to long-term success in the world of Amazon publishing.

Implementing Effective Pricing Strategies

In the fast-paced world of online entrepreneurship, one of the key factors that can make or break your success is your pricing strategy. When it comes to Amazon Publishing and Kindle Direct Publishing (KDP) authors, the importance of implementing effective pricing strategies cannot be overstated. In this subchapter, we will explore the various aspects of pricing strategies and how they can be applied to maximize your profits and reach a wider audience.

First and foremost, it is crucial to understand the market dynamics of Amazon Publishing and KDP. With millions of books available on Amazon, competition is fierce, and pricing plays a pivotal role in capturing the attention of potential customers. Setting the right price for your book can be a delicate balancing act. While you want to ensure profitability, you also need to consider factors such as demand, competition, and perceived value.

One effective pricing strategy for online entrepreneurs is dynamic pricing. This approach involves adjusting your book's price based on real-time data and market trends. By monitoring the sales performance and customer behavior, you can optimize your pricing to match the demand and maximize your revenue. Additionally, using tools such as Amazon's Sales Rank can provide valuable insights into how your book is performing in comparison to others in your niche.

Another pricing strategy worth considering is bundling. By packaging multiple books together at a discounted price, you can increase the perceived value for customers and encourage them to make a purchase. This strategy is particularly effective when you have a series of books or related titles that complement each other.

Furthermore, experimenting with different price points can help you find the sweet spot that maximizes both sales volume and profitability. Conducting A/B testing, where you offer your book at different prices to different segments of your audience, can provide valuable data on customer behavior and preferences.

Lastly, don't forget the power of promotional pricing strategies. Offering limited-time discounts or running flash sales can create a sense of urgency and drive impulse purchases. Additionally, participating in Amazon's Kindle Countdown Deals or Free Book Promotion programs can significantly boost your visibility and attract new readers.

In conclusion, implementing effective pricing strategies is vital for the success of Amazon Publishing and KDP authors. By understanding market dynamics, utilizing dynamic pricing, bundling, experimenting with different price points, and leveraging promotional pricing strategies, online entrepreneurs can maximize their profits and reach a wider audience. Remember, pricing is not a one-time decision, but an ongoing process that requires constant monitoring and adaptation to stay ahead of the competition.

Monitoring Your Sales and Adjusting Your Marketing Tactics

As an online entrepreneur or Kindle Direct Publishing (KDP) author, it is crucial to monitor your sales and continuously adjust your marketing tactics to maximize your success on Amazon Publishing. This subchapter will provide you with valuable insights and strategies to help you optimize your sales and marketing efforts on the platform.

First and foremost, it is essential to regularly monitor your sales performance on Amazon. Familiarize yourself with Amazon's sales reports and analytics tools to gain a comprehensive understanding of your book's performance. These tools will allow you to track key metrics such as unit sales, royalty earnings, and customer reviews. By closely monitoring these metrics, you can identify trends, spot opportunities, and make data-driven decisions to improve your book's visibility and sales.

One effective way to adjust your marketing tactics is by leveraging Amazon's advertising platform, Amazon Advertising. This powerful tool enables you to promote your books through various advertising options like Sponsored Products and Product Display Ads. By strategically targeting relevant keywords and categories, you can increase your book's visibility and attract more potential readers. Regularly evaluate the performance of your ads and make adjustments to optimize your return on investment.

Additionally, consider implementing different pricing strategies to boost your sales. Experiment with promotional pricing, limited-time discounts, or even offering your book for free during specific periods. These tactics can help create buzz, attract new readers, and ultimately drive more sales. Monitor the impact of these pricing strategies and adjust them accordingly to find what works best for your book and target audience.

Another crucial aspect of monitoring your sales and adjusting your marketing tactics is staying informed about industry trends and changes. Keep an eye on Amazon's policies, algorithm updates, and best practices shared by successful authors. Join online communities, forums, and social media groups dedicated to Amazon Publishing and Kindle Direct Publishing. Engage with fellow authors, share experiences, and learn from each other's strategies and insights.

In conclusion, monitoring your sales and adjusting your marketing tactics are indispensable for success as an online entrepreneur or KDP author on Amazon Publishing. By leveraging Amazon's sales reports, advertising platform, pricing strategies, and staying informed about industry trends, you can continuously optimize your book's visibility, attract more readers, and ultimately achieve your publishing goals. Stay proactive, adapt to changes, and never stop exploring new strategies to stay ahead in the competitive world of Amazon Publishing.

Chapter 8: Expanding Your Publishing Business

Creating a Series of Books

For Online Entrepreneurs and Entrepreneurs in the Amazon Publishing and Kindle Direct Publishing (KDP) authors niches, one of the most effective strategies to build a successful publishing business is by creating a series of books. A series not only allows you to create a loyal fan base but also helps in boosting your sales and increasing your visibility on Amazon.

The first step in creating a series is to decide on a theme or a genre that resonates with your target audience. Conduct thorough market research to identify popular genres and sub-genres, and choose one that aligns with your interests and expertise. This will ensure that you are passionate about the subject matter and can deliver high-quality content consistently.

Once you have decided on a theme, it's essential to plan the overall story arc for your series. Map out the major plot points and character development across the books. This will help you maintain consistency throughout the series and keep your readers engaged.

Next, focus on writing the first book in the series. This book should be able to stand alone and provide a satisfying reading experience while leaving room for further exploration in future books. Introduce compelling characters, intriguing storylines, and leave some loose ends to create anticipation for the next installment.

After publishing the first book, it's crucial to maintain a regular writing schedule to keep up the momentum. Set realistic deadlines for completing subsequent books and stick to them. Consistency is key to building a dedicated fan base who eagerly wait for each new release.

To maximize the impact of your series, leverage marketing strategies specific to book series. Create a captivating series title and design cohesive cover art that visually represents the interconnectedness of the books. Use cross-promotion techniques within your books to encourage readers to explore other titles in the series. Additionally, consider offering the first book in the series at a discounted price or even for free to entice new readers.

As your series gains popularity, actively engage with your readers by responding to reviews, hosting virtual book clubs, and seeking feedback for future installments. This will not only help you build a loyal community but also provide valuable insights for improving your writing and storytelling skills.

Creating a series of books is a powerful strategy for online entrepreneurs and entrepreneurs in the Amazon Publishing and KDP author niches. By consistently delivering high-quality content, engaging with your readers, and strategically marketing your series, you can establish yourself as a successful author and build a profitable publishing business.

Translating Your Book for International Markets

In today's globalized world, reaching international readers is a crucial step for any author or entrepreneur looking to expand their audience and increase book sales. The online marketplace, particularly Amazon Publishing and Kindle Direct Publishing (KDP, offers an excellent opportunity to tap into international markets and connect with readers from all around the world. However, to fully leverage this potential, it is essential to consider translating your book for international markets.

One of the first things to consider when translating your book is identifying the target markets. Conducting market research and understanding the demand for your genre in specific countries or regions will help you make informed decisions. Look for markets with a large English-speaking population, such as the United Kingdom, Canada, Australia, and India, as they can be great starting points for your international expansion.

Next, finding a reliable and experienced translator becomes crucial. It is important to work with someone who is not only fluent in the language but also understands the nuances and cultural context of the target market. Hiring a professional translator or working with a reputable translation agency will ensure the highest quality translation and maintain the integrity of your original work.

Once you have a translated manuscript, it is important to consider localization. Localization involves adapting your book to the local culture, customs, and preferences of the target market. This may include modifying book covers, book descriptions, or even altering certain elements of the story to make it more relatable to the local readers. Localizing your book will significantly increase its chances of success and resonate with readers in different countries.

After finalizing the translated and localized version of your book, it's time to publish it on Amazon. Take advantage of Amazon's global distribution network and select the appropriate territories for your book. By making your book available in different countries, you are increasing its visibility and accessibility to a wider audience.

Finally, marketing plays a significant role in promoting your translated book. Tailor your marketing efforts to reach the target audience in each country. Leverage social media platforms, local influencers, and book review websites to generate buzz and attract readers. Collaborating with translators or local authors can also be a great way to build relationships and gain exposure in the international market.

Translating your book for international markets can be a game-changer for your career as an author or entrepreneur. It opens up new opportunities, expands your readership, and increases your potential for success. By carefully considering the target markets, working with professional translators, localizing your content, and implementing effective marketing strategies, you can successfully navigate the global marketplace and make your mark on the international stage.

Exploring Other Publishing Platforms

Exploring Other Publishing Platforms:

In today's digital age, online entrepreneurs and authors in the Amazon Publishing and Kindle Direct Publishing (KDP) niche have witnessed the incredible power and reach of Amazon as a publishing platform. However, it is essential for ambitious entrepreneurs to explore other publishing platforms that can further expand their audience and boost their sales. This subchapter aims to introduce alternative publishing platforms and shed light on their unique benefits.

1. Smashwords: Smashwords is a popular platform that enables authors to publish and distribute their eBooks to numerous online retailers, including Apple Books, Barnes & Noble, and Kobo. With Smashwords, entrepreneurs can tap into a broader market and diversify their revenue streams while benefiting from their extensive distribution network.

2. Draft2Digital: Similar to Smashwords, Draft2Digital is another user-friendly platform that helps authors publish their eBooks across multiple online stores, such as Apple Books, Barnes & Noble, Kobo, and more. Its simplicity and comprehensive distribution network make it an appealing option for authors who want to reach a wider audience.

3. Google Play Books: Google Play Books is a prominent platform that allows entrepreneurs to publish and sell their eBooks to millions of Android users worldwide. By leveraging Google's vast user base, authors can expand their reach and potentially increase their sales significantly.

4. Lulu: Lulu is a self-publishing platform that offers authors a range of publishing services, including eBook distribution, print-on-demand, and even marketing assistance. With Lulu, entrepreneurs can have greater control over their publishing journey while exploring additional formats like print books and audiobooks.

5. Apple Books: Apple Books, formerly known as iBooks, is an excellent platform for entrepreneurs to target the vast Apple user base. By publishing on Apple Books, authors can tap into a highly engaged audience and potentially boost their sales and visibility.

While Amazon remains a critical platform for online entrepreneurs and Kindle Direct Publishing authors, exploring other publishing platforms can provide exciting opportunities for growth and diversification. By expanding their presence on different platforms, entrepreneurs can maximize their visibility, capture new readers, and increase their overall revenue.

However, it is crucial to consider the unique requirements, guidelines, and formatting standards of each platform when venturing beyond Amazon. Each platform may have its own publishing process and promotional tools, so entrepreneurs should take the time to research and adapt their strategies accordingly.

In conclusion, this subchapter encourages online entrepreneurs and Kindle Direct Publishing authors to explore other publishing platforms to expand their reach and revenue streams. By embracing alternative platforms such as Smashwords, Draft2Digital, Google Play Books, Lulu, and Apple Books, entrepreneurs can tap into new audiences, diversify their sales channels, and ultimately achieve greater success in the competitive world of online publishing.

Collaborating with Other Authors and Cross-Promotions

As an online entrepreneur and author in the world of Amazon Publishing and Kindle Direct Publishing (KDP), it is essential to understand the power of collaboration and cross-promotion with fellow authors. In this subchapter, we will delve into the strategies and benefits of working together with other authors to amplify your reach and maximize your success.

One of the most significant advantages of collaborating with other authors is the potential to tap into their existing audience. By joining forces, you can expose your work to a whole new group of readers who may be interested in your genre or niche. This cross-promotion allows you to leverage the trust and credibility that other authors have built with their readers, instantly expanding your reach and increasing your chances of gaining new fans.

There are various ways to collaborate with other authors, from joint book promotions and box sets to co-authoring projects. Joint book promotions involve teaming up with other authors to offer discounted or free books for a limited time. This strategy not only boosts sales but also generates visibility and exposure for all participating authors. Box sets, on the other hand, allow authors to bundle their books together, creating a value-packed collection that appeals to readers seeking a variety of content. Co-authoring projects involve two or more authors coming together to write a book jointly, pooling their skills, ideas, and networks to create a compelling piece of work.

When collaborating with other authors, be sure to choose partners who complement your writing style or genre. Look for authors whose readers would likely enjoy your work, and vice versa. This synergy will enhance the overall appeal of your joint projects and improve the likelihood of success.

To find potential collaborators, join author forums, online communities, and social media groups dedicated to Amazon Publishing and KDP authors. Engage with other authors, share your experiences, and explore opportunities for collaboration. Networking and establishing relationships with fellow authors will not only lead to potential partnerships but also provide valuable support and insights throughout your publishing journey.

Remember, collaboration is a two-way street. While you benefit from cross-promotion, be sure to reciprocate by promoting your collaborators' work as well. This mutual support and promotion create a win-win situation for all involved, fostering a sense of community and camaraderie among Amazon Publishing and KDP authors.

In conclusion, collaborating with other authors and engaging in cross-promotions is a powerful strategy for online entrepreneurs and authors in the realm of Amazon Publishing and KDP. By leveraging each other's audiences and expertise, you can expand your reach, increase book sales, and ultimately achieve greater success in the competitive world of self-publishing. So, embrace the power of collaboration, cultivate relationships with fellow authors, and watch your publishing career soar to new heights.

Chapter 9: Managing Your Amazon Publishing Business

Tracking Sales and Royalties

As an online entrepreneur or author in the field of Amazon publishing or Kindle Direct Publishing (KDP), it is crucial to have a clear understanding of how your sales and royalties are being tracked. This subchapter will provide you with the ultimate guide to effectively track your sales and royalties, enabling you to optimize your strategies and maximize your profits.

One of the key tools for tracking sales and royalties is the Amazon Author Central platform. This powerful platform provides you with valuable insights into your book sales, allowing you to monitor your progress and identify trends. Through Amazon Author Central, you can view your sales data in real-time, analyze your best-selling book categories, and track your royalties. This information is crucial for making informed decisions about your marketing efforts and identifying the most profitable areas of your business.

Another important aspect of tracking sales and royalties is understanding the royalty structure of Amazon publishing. Amazon offers different royalty rates depending on the pricing and distribution options you choose. By familiarizing yourself with the royalty structure, you can determine the most profitable pricing strategy for your books and optimize your earnings. This subchapter will provide you with a detailed breakdown of the royalty rates and how they are calculated, ensuring you have a comprehensive understanding of your potential earnings.

In addition to Amazon Author Central, there are various third-party tracking tools available that can provide you with more advanced analytics and insights. These tools allow you to delve deeper into your sales data, track keywords and rankings, and monitor the performance of your competitors. By leveraging these tools, you can gain a competitive edge in the Amazon publishing market and fine-tune your strategies based on data-driven insights.

Finally, this subchapter will also cover the importance of tracking sales and royalties for tax purposes. As an entrepreneur, it is essential to keep accurate records of your earnings and expenses to ensure compliance with tax regulations. By implementing effective tracking systems, you can streamline your financial reporting and simplify the tax filing process.

In conclusion, tracking sales and royalties is a crucial aspect of running a successful Amazon publishing or Kindle Direct Publishing (KDP) business. By utilizing platforms like Amazon Author Central, understanding the royalty structure, leveraging third-party tracking tools, and managing your finances effectively, you can optimize your strategies, maximize your profits, and achieve long-term success in the competitive world of online publishing.

Understanding Amazon's Terms and Policies

As an online entrepreneur or entrepreneur in the Amazon Publishing or Kindle Direct Publishing (KDP) author niches, it is vital to have a solid grasp of Amazon's terms and policies. This subchapter aims to provide you with a comprehensive understanding of these terms and policies to help you navigate the Amazon platform effectively and maximize your success as an Amazon publisher.

Amazon's terms and policies form the foundation of the platform and are designed to maintain a fair and transparent marketplace for both buyers and sellers. By familiarizing yourself with these guidelines, you can ensure compliance, avoid penalties, and create a positive experience for your readers and customers.

One of the key areas to focus on is Amazon's content guidelines. These guidelines outline what is acceptable and what is not in terms of the content you publish. Understanding these guidelines will help you avoid potential copyright infringements, offensive material, and other violations that could result in your book being removed from the platform.

Additionally, it is crucial to understand Amazon's pricing and royalty policies. These policies determine how much you earn per sale and what pricing strategies are allowed. By familiarizing yourself with these policies, you can optimize your pricing to maximize profits and balance competitive pricing with profitability.

Another essential aspect is Amazon's reviews and ratings policies. These policies outline what is considered acceptable behavior when it comes to soliciting reviews, dealing with negative reviews, and reporting suspicious activities. Understanding these policies will help you build a strong reputation, enhance customer trust, and avoid penalties for unethical practices.

Furthermore, Amazon's terms and policies cover various other areas such as intellectual property rights, advertising guidelines, and customer service requirements. By delving into these sections, you can ensure you are abiding by the rules and regulations set by Amazon, thereby protecting your brand and preserving a positive relationship with the platform.

In conclusion, comprehending Amazon's terms and policies is of utmost importance for online entrepreneurs and entrepreneurs in the Amazon Publishing and KDP author niches. By understanding and adhering to these guidelines, you can navigate the platform confidently, avoid penalties, and create a successful publishing journey on Amazon.

Dealing with Copyright and Intellectual Property Issues

In the fast-paced world of online entrepreneurship, protecting your intellectual property is crucial. As an Amazon Publishing or Kindle Direct Publishing (KDP) author, you need to be aware of the potential copyright and intellectual property issues that can arise. This subchapter will guide you through the essentials of dealing with these issues, ensuring that your creative work remains safe and profitable.

Understanding Copyright Basics

To effectively navigate the world of copyright and intellectual property, it is essential to grasp the basics. This includes understanding what copyright protects, how it is obtained, and the length of its protection. We will explore the nuances of copyright for different types of creative works, such as books, illustrations, and photographs. By gaining a solid understanding of copyright, you can safeguard your work and prevent others from unlawfully using or profiting from it.

Registering Your Copyright

While copyright protection is automatic upon creation, registering your copyright provides additional benefits and legal advantages. We will delve into the process of copyright registration and explain why it is a wise investment for authors and entrepreneurs. By registering your copyright, you establish a public record of ownership, making it easier to enforce your rights and claim damages in case of infringement.

Avoiding Copyright Infringement

As an online entrepreneur, it is crucial to respect the intellectual property rights of others. We will outline strategies for avoiding copyright infringement, such as conducting thorough research, obtaining permissions, and properly attributing sources. By following these guidelines, you can create a successful business without running into legal disputes that could tarnish your reputation and financial standing.

Protecting Your Intellectual Property

Beyond copyright, we will explore additional ways to protect your intellectual property. This includes trademarks, patents, and trade secrets. We will explain how these forms of protection differ from copyright and how they can be utilized to safeguard your brand, inventions, and proprietary information.

Enforcing Your Rights

Even with preventive measures in place, copyright and intellectual property disputes can still arise. We will provide practical advice on how to enforce your rights, whether through cease and desist letters, negotiation, or legal action. Understanding the steps involved in resolving such disputes will empower you to protect your creative work and maintain a profitable business.

Conclusion

Dealing with copyright and intellectual property issues is an integral part of being a successful online entrepreneur, especially for Amazon Publishing and KDP authors. By understanding copyright basics, registering your copyright, avoiding infringement, protecting your intellectual property, and knowing how to enforce your rights, you can navigate this complex landscape with confidence.

Managing Customer Reviews and Feedback

As an online entrepreneur, particularly if you are an Amazon Publishing or Kindle Direct Publishing (KDP) author, managing customer reviews and feedback is crucial for the success of your business. Customer reviews and feedback play a significant role in shaping your reputation, brand image, and ultimately, your sales. This subchapter will guide you on how to effectively manage customer reviews and feedback, ensuring a positive and fruitful relationship with your customers.

First and foremost, it is essential to understand the importance of customer reviews. Reviews act as social proof and influence potential customers' purchase decisions. Positive reviews not only boost your credibility but also increase the likelihood of attracting new customers. Conversely, negative reviews can harm your reputation and deter potential buyers. Therefore, it is crucial to actively manage and respond to customer reviews.

One of the key strategies for managing customer reviews is to encourage and facilitate feedback. Ensure that you provide an easy and accessible platform for customers to leave reviews. Consider including a call-to-action in your product descriptions or emails, urging customers to share their experiences. Additionally, promptly respond to customer reviews, both positive and negative, to show that you value their feedback and are committed to addressing any concerns.

When responding to negative reviews, it is important to remain professional and empathetic. Address the customer's concerns and offer solutions or alternatives. This not only shows your commitment to customer satisfaction but also demonstrates to potential customers that you take feedback seriously and are willing to go the extra mile to rectify any issues.

Furthermore, monitor your product's reviews and ratings regularly. By staying up-to-date with feedback, you can identify patterns or recurring issues that need your attention. Implementing necessary changes based on customer feedback can significantly improve the quality and desirability of your products, leading to increased sales and customer satisfaction.

Lastly, consider leveraging positive reviews as marketing tools. Highlighting positive customer testimonials on your product pages or social media platforms can instill confidence in potential buyers and increase conversion rates.

In conclusion, managing customer reviews and feedback is a critical aspect of running a successful online business, especially in the realm of Amazon Publishing and Kindle Direct Publishing. By actively encouraging feedback, responding promptly and professionally to reviews, and implementing necessary changes based on customer insights, you can build a positive reputation, attract new customers, and ultimately boost your sales. Remember, customer feedback is an invaluable asset that can fuel your business growth and success.

Chapter 10: Advanced Strategies for Success

Building a Brand as an Author

In today's digital age, building a brand as an author is crucial for success in the Amazon publishing industry. With thousands of books being published every day, it is essential to stand out from the crowd and establish yourself as an authority in your niche. This subchapter will guide online entrepreneurs and entrepreneurs in the Amazon Publishing and Kindle Direct Publishing (KDP) niche on how to build and strengthen their author brand.

First and foremost, understanding your target audience is key. Research and identify the readers who resonate with your genre and writing style. By knowing their preferences, you can tailor your brand to attract and engage them effectively. Develop a unique voice and writing style that sets you apart from other authors in your genre.

Creating a compelling author bio is another vital aspect of building your brand. Your bio should reflect your personality, expertise, and passion for writing. It should also highlight any relevant achievements, such as awards or previous publications, to establish credibility. Remember to update your bio regularly to reflect any new accomplishments or changes in your writing career.

Consistency is crucial in building a brand. Ensure that your book covers, author photos, and promotional materials have a consistent theme and design. This visual identity will help readers recognize and remember your brand. Consider hiring a professional designer to create visually appealing and cohesive branding elements.

Building an online presence is essential in today's digital world. Create an author website and regularly update it with engaging content, such as blog posts, author interviews, or book reviews. Utilize social media platforms to connect with your target audience and share updates about your writing journey. Engage in conversations, respond to comments, and foster a sense of community around your brand.

Engaging with your readers is crucial for building a strong author brand. Encourage readers to leave reviews and feedback on your books. Interact with them on social media platforms, respond to their messages and comments, and show genuine appreciation for their support. By forging a personal connection with your readers, you can develop a loyal fan base that will eagerly await your future releases.

Lastly, consider collaborating with other authors or influencers in your genre. Cross-promotions, guest blogging, or joint events can help expand your reach and introduce your brand to new readers.

In conclusion, building a brand as an author is essential for success in the Amazon publishing industry. By understanding your target audience, creating a compelling author bio, maintaining consistency in your branding, building an online presence, engaging with readers, and collaborating with others, you can establish a strong and recognizable author brand. Remember, building a brand takes time and effort, but the rewards are worth it in the long run.

Leveraging Amazon's Author Central

In today's digital age, Amazon has become synonymous with online shopping and e-commerce. However, what many people may not realize is that Amazon is also a major player in the publishing industry. With the advent of Kindle Direct Publishing (KDP), authors now have an unprecedented opportunity to self-publish their books and reach a global audience. To truly maximize your potential as an author on Amazon, it is essential to understand and leverage the power of Amazon's Author Central.

Amazon's Author Central is a free service that allows authors to create a dedicated profile page on Amazon. This page serves as a hub for all of your books, making it easier for readers to discover and connect with your work. It also provides valuable insights into your book sales, customer reviews, and author rankings, allowing you to track and measure your success.

One of the key benefits of utilizing Amazon's Author Central is the ability to personalize your author profile. With a compelling author bio, professional headshot, and links to your website or social media accounts, you can establish a strong online presence and build credibility with your readers. By making your profile engaging and informative, you can increase reader engagement and foster a loyal fan base.

Another powerful feature of Author Central is the ability to add editorial reviews to your book listings. These reviews can be obtained from reputable sources such as industry experts, fellow authors, or book reviewers. By showcasing positive reviews on your book's page, you can enhance its visibility and appeal to potential buyers. This can greatly influence purchasing decisions and ultimately boost your sales.

In addition to personalizing your profile and adding editorial reviews, Amazon's Author Central also offers promotional tools to help you increase your book's visibility. Through programs like Kindle Countdown Deals and Kindle Free Book Promotions, you can run limited-time discounts or offer your book for free to attract new readers and generate buzz. By strategically leveraging these promotions and effectively marketing your book, you can significantly boost your sales and increase your revenue.

In conclusion, if you are an online entrepreneur or an aspiring author in the Amazon Publishing or Kindle Direct Publishing (KDP) niche, understanding and leveraging Amazon's Author Central is essential. By creating a compelling author profile, showcasing positive reviews, and utilizing promotional tools, you can maximize your book's visibility, engage with readers, and ultimately achieve success in the highly competitive world of self-publishing on Amazon.

Diversifying Your Income Streams

In today's fast-paced and ever-evolving digital landscape, it has become increasingly important for online entrepreneurs, particularly those in the Amazon Publishing and Kindle Direct Publishing (KDP) niches, to diversify their income streams. While Amazon Publishing and KDP offer fantastic opportunities for authors and entrepreneurs to generate revenue, relying solely on these platforms can be risky. By diversifying your income streams, you can safeguard your financial stability and maximize your earning potential.

One of the most effective ways to diversify your income streams is by expanding your presence on multiple platforms. While Amazon Publishing and KDP may be your bread and butter, there are numerous other online marketplaces and platforms where you can showcase your work. Consider exploring other e-book retailers such as Barnes & Noble, Kobo, or Apple Books. Additionally, don't underestimate the power of audiobooks and print-on-demand services. By making your content available in various formats, you can reach a broader audience and tap into new revenue streams.

Another strategy for diversifying your income streams is by leveraging your intellectual property. As an author or entrepreneur, you possess a valuable asset – your content. Consider licensing your work for translation into different languages, or explore opportunities for film or television adaptations. By exploring these avenues, you can generate additional income and expose your work to new audiences.

Furthermore, don't underestimate the potential of affiliate marketing. As an online entrepreneur, you likely have a strong network and audience base. Partnering with relevant brands and promoting their products or services through affiliate marketing can be an excellent way to earn passive income. This strategy allows you to monetize your existing audience and diversify your income streams without creating additional content.

Lastly, consider developing additional revenue streams through teaching or coaching. As an established author or entrepreneur, you possess valuable knowledge and expertise that others are willing to pay for. Create online courses, offer one-on-one coaching sessions, or host webinars to share your insights and help others achieve their goals. Not only will this diversify your income, but it will also establish you as an authority in your field.

In conclusion, diversifying your income streams is crucial for online entrepreneurs in the Amazon Publishing and KDP niches. By expanding your presence on multiple platforms, leveraging your intellectual property, embracing affiliate marketing, and exploring teaching or coaching opportunities, you can safeguard your financial stability and maximize your earning potential. Remember, the key to success lies in not putting all your eggs in one basket.

Staying Updated with Industry Trends and Best Practices

In the ever-evolving world of online entrepreneurship, it is crucial to stay updated with industry trends and best practices to remain competitive and successful. This subchapter aims to provide valuable insights and strategies for online entrepreneurs, specifically those involved in Amazon Publishing and Kindle Direct Publishing (KDP) authors. By staying on top of industry trends and adopting best practices, you can maximize your chances of success and ensure sustainable growth in your online business.

The publishing landscape is constantly changing, driven by consumer demand and advancements in technology. As an online entrepreneur in the Amazon Publishing space, it is essential to stay updated with the latest trends and innovations. This subchapter will explore various sources to gather industry insights, such as industry publications, forums, social media groups, and attending relevant conferences and events. By regularly consuming these resources, you can gain a comprehensive understanding of the current market dynamics and identify emerging opportunities.

Furthermore, this subchapter will delve into the significance of best practices in Amazon Publishing and KDP. It will discuss the importance of optimizing book descriptions, keywords, and categories to enhance discoverability and increase sales. It will also emphasize the need to consistently monitor and analyze sales data to identify trends, tweak marketing strategies, and adapt to changing consumer preferences. Additionally, it will highlight the significance of building a strong author brand and engaging with readers through various channels, such as author websites, social media, and email newsletters.

Moreover, this subchapter will emphasize the value of networking and collaboration within the Amazon Publishing and KDP community. By connecting with fellow entrepreneurs and authors, you can exchange knowledge, share experiences, and learn from each other's successes and failures. Collaborative efforts, such as cross-promotions and joint ventures, can also amplify your reach and attract a wider audience.

Finally, this subchapter will stress the importance of continuous learning and professional development. It will provide recommendations for books, courses, and online resources that can help you improve your writing skills, marketing strategies, and overall business acumen.

In conclusion, staying updated with industry trends and best practices is vital for online entrepreneurs, especially those involved in Amazon Publishing and Kindle Direct Publishing. By staying informed, adopting best practices, and networking within the community, you can position yourself for long-term success and growth in the dynamic world of online entrepreneurship.

Chapter 11: Case Studies from Successful Amazon Authors

Author A: How I Made a Bestseller on Amazon

Subchapter: Author A: How I Made a Bestseller on Amazon

Introduction:
In this subchapter, we will delve into the inspiring journey of Author A, who managed to achieve the coveted status of a best-selling author on Amazon. This chapter aims to provide valuable insights and practical tips for online entrepreneurs and Kindle Direct Publishing (KDP) authors looking to replicate Author A's success. By understanding the strategies and mindset behind Author A's achievement, readers can discover the key elements necessary for making their own mark on Amazon's vast publishing platform.

Author A's Background:
Before becoming a best-selling author, Author A faced numerous challenges and setbacks in their writing career. However, they persevered and eventually found their breakthrough on Amazon's platform. By sharing their story, Author A offers aspiring authors and online entrepreneurs a glimpse into the realities of the publishing world and the potential for success through Amazon.

Identifying a Profitable Niche:
One of the crucial factors that contributed to Author A's success was their ability to identify a profitable niche. We will explore how Author A conducted thorough market research and identified a gap in the market that allowed them to cater to a specific audience's needs. By understanding the importance of niche selection, readers will be able to strategically position their own books for success on Amazon.

Crafting an Engaging Book:

Author A's journey to a bestseller was not solely based on marketing tactics but also on the quality of their book. We will delve into the process of how Author A meticulously crafted a compelling and engaging book that resonated with their target audience. From developing a captivating storyline to creating relatable characters, readers will gain valuable insights into the art of writing a book that stands out among the crowd.

Effective Marketing Strategies:

In this subchapter, we will uncover the marketing strategies that propelled Author A's book to the top of Amazon's charts. From leveraging social media platforms and building an author platform to utilizing Amazon's promotional tools, readers will learn how to effectively market their books and gain visibility in the competitive Amazon marketplace.

Building a Long-term Author Brand:

Author A's success did not stop with one best-selling book. They were able to build a sustainable author brand that continues to attract readers and generate sales. We will explore the strategies Author A employed to maintain their success and expand their reach beyond Amazon's platform, such as building an email list, engaging with readers, and developing a content marketing strategy.

Conclusion:

Author A's journey from struggling writer to best-selling author on Amazon serves as an inspiration for online entrepreneurs and Kindle Direct Publishing (KDP) authors. By understanding their strategies, mindset, and attention to detail, readers will be equipped with the tools necessary to make their own mark on Amazon's publishing platform. Whether you are a budding author or an online entrepreneur looking to tap into the potential of Amazon, this subchapter will provide you with valuable insights to achieve success in the world of Amazon publishing.

Author B: From Unknown to Kindle Millionaire

In the ever-evolving world of self-publishing, there are countless success stories that inspire and motivate aspiring authors. One such tale is that of Author B, who went from being an unknown writer to a Kindle millionaire through Amazon Publishing. This subchapter delves into the journey of Author B, offering valuable insights and lessons for online entrepreneurs looking to make it big in the world of Kindle Direct Publishing (KDP).

Author B's story is a testament to the power of perseverance, determination, and effective marketing strategies. Like many aspiring authors, Author B started with a dream and a manuscript, unsure of how to navigate the complex world of publishing. However, armed with the right knowledge and tools, Author B was able to turn their book into a bestseller.

This subchapter sheds light on the step-by-step process that Author B followed to achieve their tremendous success. It begins by exploring the importance of conducting thorough market research and identifying profitable niches within the Amazon Publishing landscape. Through careful analysis and understanding of target readers, Author B was able to craft a book that resonated with a wide audience.

Furthermore, the subchapter delves into the various techniques and strategies that Author B employed to promote their book effectively. From leveraging social media platforms to building an email list and running targeted advertising campaigns, Author B left no stone unturned in their quest for success. The chapter highlights the importance of building a robust author platform and developing a strong online presence, which proved to be crucial in Author B's rise to stardom.

Moreover, this subchapter offers practical tips and advice for online entrepreneurs who aspire to replicate Author B's success. It discusses the significance of investing in professional cover design, editing, and formatting to ensure the highest quality product. Additionally, it emphasizes the importance of continuously honing one's writing skills and staying up-to-date with trends and developments in the publishing industry.

Author B's journey from an unknown writer to a Kindle millionaire is an inspiration for all online entrepreneurs and authors in the Amazon Publishing and Kindle Direct Publishing (KDP) niches. This subchapter serves as a guide, providing valuable insights and strategies that can propel aspiring authors towards achieving their dreams. By learning from Author B's experiences and implementing the strategies outlined, online entrepreneurs can increase their chances of making it big in the world of self-publishing.

Author C: Niche Publishing and Targeted Marketing

In the world of Amazon publishing, there is a vast sea of books and authors vying for attention. It can be a daunting task for any author, especially those who are new to the game. That's where niche publishing and targeted marketing come into play. In this subchapter, we will delve into the strategies and techniques that Author C has employed to carve out a successful niche in Amazon Publishing.

Author C understands the power of finding a specific niche and catering to a targeted audience. By focusing on a particular genre or subject matter, Author C has been able to establish themselves as an expert in their field. This not only helps them stand out from the competition but also allows them to connect with a passionate and engaged readership.

One of the key aspects of niche publishing is understanding your target market. Author C knows their readers inside out and has taken the time to research and understand their preferences, interests, and pain points. This knowledge has allowed them to craft books that resonate with their audience on a deep level, resulting in higher sales and positive reviews.

But it doesn't stop there. Author C has also mastered the art of targeted marketing. They know that simply writing a great book is not enough; it needs to reach the right audience. Through strategic marketing campaigns, Author C has been able to put their books in front of the eyes of their ideal readers, ensuring maximum visibility and sales.

One of the tools that Author C has utilized is Kindle Direct Publishing (KDP). This platform allows authors to self-publish their work and reach millions of readers worldwide. Author C has taken full advantage of the features and benefits offered by KDP, using it as a springboard to success.

In this subchapter, Author C will share their strategies for finding a niche, understanding the target market, and implementing effective marketing techniques. They will provide practical tips and actionable advice that can be applied by online entrepreneurs and entrepreneurs in the Amazon Publishing and KDP author niches.

By the end of this subchapter, readers will have a clear roadmap for how to identify a niche, cultivate a loyal readership, and market their books to the right audience. Author C's insights and experiences will empower online entrepreneurs and entrepreneurs to thrive in the competitive world of Amazon Publishing.

Chapter 12: Conclusion and Next Steps

Recap of Key Takeaways

As an online entrepreneur or entrepreneur looking to dive into the world of Amazon Publishing and Kindle Direct Publishing (KDP), it's crucial to understand the key takeaways from this comprehensive guide. In this subchapter, we will recap the most important points covered throughout the book, ensuring you have a solid foundation to succeed in your publishing journey.

1. Embrace the Power of Amazon Publishing: Amazon is the largest online marketplace in the world, and publishing your book through their platform gives you access to a massive customer base. Recognize the potential of this platform and leverage it to reach a wider audience and boost your sales.

2. Understand the Kindle Direct Publishing (KDP) Process: Kindle Direct Publishing is Amazon's self-publishing platform, allowing authors to publish their books in digital format. Familiarize yourself with the process, from creating an account to formatting your manuscript, designing a compelling cover, and pricing your book effectively.

3. Craft a Captivating Book Description: Your book description is a vital marketing tool. Focus on creating a concise, engaging, and persuasive description that entices potential readers to click the "Buy Now" button. Highlight the unique selling points of your book and use compelling language to generate interest.

4. Utilize Effective Strategies for Book Promotion: Merely publishing your book on Amazon is not enough; you need to actively promote it to increase visibility and sales. Explore various marketing strategies, such as book

giveaways, social media campaigns, email marketing, collaborations with influencers, and paid advertising, to expand your reach and attract readers.

5. Master the Art of Keywords and Categories: Properly optimizing your book's metadata is crucial for visibility on Amazon. Conduct thorough keyword research to identify relevant and high-traffic keywords, and strategically place them in your book title, subtitle, description, and backend keywords. Additionally, choose the most appropriate categories and subcategories to increase your book's discoverability.

6. Continuously Gather and Incorporate Reader Feedback: Embrace constructive criticism and use it to improve your future work. Encourage readers to leave reviews and ratings, and actively engage with them through author notes and updates. Listen to their feedback, address any concerns, and make necessary changes to enhance the reader experience.

7. Stay Informed and Adapt to Changing Trends: The publishing industry, especially in the digital realm, is constantly evolving. Stay up-to-date with the latest trends, changes in algorithms, and new marketing techniques. Be adaptable and willing to experiment to stay ahead of the competition and maximize your success.

By internalizing these key takeaways, you are equipped with the knowledge and insights needed to thrive as an Amazon Publishing and KDP author. Remember, success in the publishing world requires dedication, perseverance, and continuous learning. Now, go forth and conquer the world of Amazon Publishing with confidence!

Planning Your Publishing Journey

As an online entrepreneur or entrepreneur looking to venture into the world of Amazon publishing, it is crucial to have a well-thought-out plan in order to maximize your chances of success. This subchapter, "Planning Your Publishing Journey," aims to provide you with the necessary insights and guidance to navigate the intricacies of Amazon Publishing and Kindle Direct Publishing (KDP).

The first step in planning your publishing journey is to define your goals and objectives. Ask yourself what you hope to achieve through publishing on Amazon. Are you looking to establish yourself as an authority in your niche, generate passive income, or promote your existing products or services? Clearly identifying your goals will help you make informed decisions throughout the publishing process.

Next, it is vital to conduct thorough market research. Familiarize yourself with the Amazon marketplace and understand the demand for your chosen niche. Analyze the competition, identify gaps in the market, and explore potential target audiences. This research will enable you to position your book effectively and tailor your content to meet your readers' specific needs.

Once you have a clear understanding of your goals and the market, it is time to focus on the writing process. Develop a writing schedule that works for you and commit to it. Whether you decide to write the book yourself or hire a ghostwriter, adhering to a schedule will ensure steady progress.

While writing, pay attention to the formatting and structure of your book. Amazon Publishing and KDP have specific guidelines that you need to follow to ensure your book meets their quality standards. Take the time to familiarize yourself with these guidelines and apply them to your manuscript.

Simultaneously, consider your book's cover design, title, and book description. These elements play a crucial role in attracting potential readers and convincing them to purchase your book. Invest in professional cover design and craft a compelling title and description that accurately represents your content.

After completing your manuscript, it is time to enter the publishing phase. Familiarize yourself with the publishing options available on Amazon, such as

Kindle Direct Publishing (KDP). Understand the different publishing formats and select the one that aligns with your goals and target audience.

Finally, devise a marketing and promotion strategy for your book. Amazon's marketplace is vast, and it is essential to stand out among the competition. Consider utilizing social media, email marketing, book reviews, and Amazon's own advertising platform to reach your target audience effectively.

In conclusion, planning your publishing journey is a critical step towards achieving success as an Amazon Publishing or Kindle Direct Publishing author. By setting clear goals, conducting thorough market research, focusing on the writing process, adhering to quality standards, and implementing effective marketing strategies, you can maximize your chances of reaching your target audience and achieving your publishing goals.

Resources and Tools for Amazon Authors

As an online entrepreneur or an entrepreneur looking to tap into the vast potential of Amazon Publishing and Kindle Direct Publishing (KDP), it is crucial to have the right resources and tools at your disposal. This subchapter aims to provide you with a comprehensive list of resources and tools that will help you navigate the world of Amazon Publishing and optimize your chances of success.

1. Amazon KDP: This is the primary platform for self-publishing on Amazon. It allows you to create, publish, and manage your books in both digital and print formats. Take advantage of the numerous features offered by KDP, such as Kindle Unlimited, Kindle Countdown Deals, and Kindle MatchBook. Familiarize yourself with the KDP dashboard, where you can track your sales and royalties.

2. Kindlepreneur: This website is a treasure trove of resources for Amazon authors. From keyword research tools to book marketing strategies, Kindlepreneur offers valuable insights to help you boost your book's visibility

and sales. Don't miss their Kindle Calculator, which helps you estimate the potential earnings of your book.

3. Book Cover Design Tools: A visually appealing book cover can make a significant difference in attracting readers. Use tools like Canva or Adobe Spark to design professional-looking book covers that grab attention and convey the essence of your book.

4. Kindlepreneur's AMS Ads Course: If you're interested in leveraging Amazon's advertising platform, Kindlepreneur's AMS Ads Course is a must-have. It provides step-by-step guidance on setting up and optimizing your Amazon ads, ensuring that your books reach the right audience.

5. Grammarly: Good writing is essential for success in the publishing world. Grammarly is an invaluable tool that helps you identify grammar and spelling errors, improve sentence structure, and enhance the overall quality of your writing.

6. Publisher Rocket: This software provides valuable insights into the Amazon marketplace, helping you identify profitable book niches, analyze competitor data, and optimize your book's metadata. Publisher Rocket saves you time and effort in market research, allowing you to focus on writing and publishing.

7. Kindle Spy: Another powerful tool for market research, Kindle Spy provides in-depth analysis of Amazon's best-selling books, their sales ranks, and estimated revenue. Use this information to gain a competitive edge and identify lucrative opportunities.

By utilizing these resources and tools, you can streamline your Amazon Publishing journey and increase your chances of success. Remember, staying informed, continuously learning, and adapting to the ever-changing landscape of Amazon Publishing is key to achieving your entrepreneurial goals in this niche.

Final Thoughts and Encouragement for Entrepreneurs

Congratulations! You've made it to the end of "The Ultimate Guide to Amazon Publishing: A Must-Have for Entrepreneurs." Throughout this book, we have explored the ins and outs of Amazon Publishing and Kindle Direct Publishing (KDP), providing you with the knowledge and tools necessary to succeed in the world of online entrepreneurship. As we wrap up this journey, we would like to leave you with some final thoughts and words of encouragement.

First and foremost, remember that entrepreneurship is not for the faint of heart. It requires dedication, perseverance, and the willingness to take risks. Building a successful business, whether it's through Amazon Publishing or any other avenue, takes time and effort. Don't be discouraged by setbacks or challenges along the way. Instead, view them as opportunities for growth and learning.

One of the key takeaways from this book is the importance of staying up-to-date with the ever-changing landscape of online entrepreneurship. Amazon Publishing and KDP are constantly evolving, and it's crucial to keep yourself informed about new strategies, trends, and tools. Join industry forums, attend conferences, and network with fellow entrepreneurs to stay ahead of the game.

Additionally, never underestimate the power of continuous improvement. As an entrepreneur, your success is directly tied to your ability to adapt and innovate. Be open to feedback and constructive criticism, and always be on the lookout for ways to improve your products, marketing techniques, and customer service. Embrace a growth mindset and never settle for mediocrity.

Finally, surround yourself with like-minded individuals who share your passion for entrepreneurship. Building a supportive network of fellow Amazon Publishing and KDP authors can provide you with valuable insights, motivation, and inspiration. Seek out mentors who have already achieved success in your niche and learn from their experiences. Remember, success is rarely achieved alone.

In conclusion, embarking on the journey of entrepreneurship is both exciting and challenging. "The Ultimate Guide to Amazon Publishing: A Must-Have for Entrepreneurs" has equipped you with the necessary knowledge and tools to navigate the world of online entrepreneurship successfully. As you move forward, keep in mind the importance of perseverance, continuous learning, and building a strong network. With dedication and the right mindset, you have the power to achieve great things in the realm of Amazon Publishing and beyond. Good luck on your entrepreneurial journey!